A Guide to AMERICAN STATES

Maine

THE PINE TREE STATE

MEDIA ENHANCED BOOKS
AV²
BY WEIGL
ADDED VALUE • AUDIO VISUAL

www.av2books.com

AV² provides enriched content that supplements and complements this book. Weigl's AV² books strive to create inspired learning and engage young minds in a total learning experience.

Your AV² Media Enhanced books come alive with...

Audio
Listen to sections of the book read aloud.

Key Words
Study vocabulary, and complete a matching word activity.

Video
Watch informative video clips.

Quizzes
Test your knowledge.

Embedded Weblinks
Gain additional information for research.

Slide Show
View images and captions, and prepare a presentation.

Try This!
Complete activities and hands-on experiments.

... and much, much more!

Go to **www.av2books.com**, and enter this book's unique code.

BOOK CODE

T765764

AV² by Weigl brings you media enhanced books that support active learning.

Published by AV² by Weigl
350 5th Avenue, 59th Floor
New York, NY 10118
Website: www.av2books.com   www.weigl.com

Library of Congress Cataloging-in-Publication Data

Foran, Jill.
 Maine / Jill Foran.
    p. cm. -- (A guide to American states)
 Includes index.
 ISBN 978-1-61690-791-4 (hardcover : alk. paper) -- ISBN 978-1-61690-467-8 (online)
 1. Maine--Juvenile literature. I. Title.
 F19.3.F665 2011
 974.1--dc23
                        2011018331

Printed in the United States of America in North Mankato, Minnesota

052011
WEP180511

Project Coordinator Jordan McGill
Art Director Terry Paulhus

Photo Credits
Every reasonable effort has been made to trace ownership and to obtain permission to reprint copyright material. The publishers would be pleased to have any errors or omissions brought to their attention so that they may be corrected in subsequent printings.

Weigl acknowledges Getty Images as its primary image supplier for this title.
Image on page 20 (right) is printed courtesy of Maine Maritime Museum, Bath, Maine.

Contents

AV² Book Code..............................2

Introduction................................4

Where Is Maine?..........................6

Mapping Maine............................8

The Land...................................10

Climate......................................12

Natural Resources.....................14

Plants.......................................16

Animals.....................................18

Tourism.....................................20

Industry....................................22

Goods and Services...................24

American Indians......................26

Explorers...................................28

Early Settlers.............................30

Notable People..........................32

Population.................................34

Politics and Government............36

Cultural Groups.........................38

Arts and Entertainment.............40

Sports.......................................42

National Averages Comparison...44

How to Improve My Community...45

Exercise Your Mind!..................46

Words to Know / Index..............47

Log on to www.av2books.com...48

Maine's annual lobster catch is the largest in the nation.

Introduction

Throughout history Maine's thick forests and abundant ocean life have supported the inhabitants of the area. Early American Indians hunted in the forests and fished the rivers, lakes, and coastal waters. When Europeans arrived in what is now Maine, the region's resources helped them establish profitable trapping and fishing industries as well as successful lumber and shipbuilding companies.

Early explorers included the Spanish, the English, and possibly even the Vikings, but it was the French who probably first tried to settle the area, in 1604. The colony moved to Nova Scotia shortly thereafter. During the 1620s several permanent English settlements were founded. Some people believe that the name Maine may have been chosen to

Jordan Pond is part of Acadia National Park, one of the country's beautiful unspoiled natural areas.

Maine trees are used to build houses and make furniture, paper, and other products. Estimates say each American consumes about one 100-foot tree a year.

distinguish the mainland settlements from the island settlements. By the mid-1800s thousands of people from other states and immigrants from different parts of Europe had come to Maine to take advantage of its natural riches. Many came to work in mills and plants that produced goods such as paper, textiles, shoes, and foodstuffs. Maine's resources were responsible for the growth of both its economy and its population.

Maine is nicknamed the Pine Tree State. This is because towering pine trees once dominated Maine's forests. Many pine trees were cut down in the 1700s and 1800s for use in the lumber and shipbuilding industries. Maine's nickname is still fitting, as there are now many second-growth pine trees in the state. Forestry continues to be an important industry, and there are many sawmills and lumber camps.

Where Is Maine?

As the largest state among the six in New England, Maine is something like the "big fish in a small pond." The state is not only the most northeastern state in New England, it is the most northeastern state in the entire nation. About 500 years ago Maine's location made it a prime fishing and trading destination for explorers. Today fishing is still important to the area. Due to its proximity to the Atlantic Ocean, the state has one of the largest annual ocean catches in the nation.

Today Maine has more than 60 lighthouses along its shore. They were originally built to guide ships.

Along with the large catches off the Atlantic coast, Maine is also known for its beautiful coastline, which is nearly 3,500 miles long. Charming fishing towns and beautiful beaches grace its shore. There are also many rocky outcroppings and islands that made navigating the coast very tricky and dangerous in Maine's early days.

There are a number of ways to get to Maine. The largest and busiest airport in the state is Portland International Jetport. For those traveling by automobile, a number of highways link the state to other parts of the country. One of the busiest highways in Maine is Interstate 95. Although passenger trains do not serve Maine, several bus lines bring passengers to various points in the state. Maine can also be reached by water. Ferries provide service to many of Maine's ports along the Atlantic Ocean.

I DIDN'T KNOW THAT!

Maine covers more than 30,800 square miles of land.

Maine is the only state in the Union that borders on only one other state. That state is New Hampshire.

Eastport is the most eastern city in the United States. People in Eastport see the morning sun before anyone else in the country.

Maine is the only state in the country whose name has just one syllable.

Private and state-run ferries provide a vital link to Maine's many island communities.

Mapping MAINE

Maine shares more of its border with Canadian provinces than it does with other states. The province of Quebec borders Maine to the northwest, and the province of New Brunswick borders it to the northeast. Maine shares its western border with the state of New Hampshire, and its entire southern border hugs the Atlantic Ocean.

Sites and Symbols

STATE SEAL
Maine

STATE BIRD
Chickadee

STATE FLOWER
White Pine Cone and Tassel

STATE FLAG
Maine

STATE ANIMAL
Moose

STATE TREE
White Pine

Nickname The Pine Tree State

Motto *Dirigo* (I Direct)

Song "State of Maine Song," words and music by Roger Vinton Snow

Entered the Union March 15, 1820, as the 23rd state

Capital Augusta

Population (2010 Census) 1,328,361 Ranked 41st state

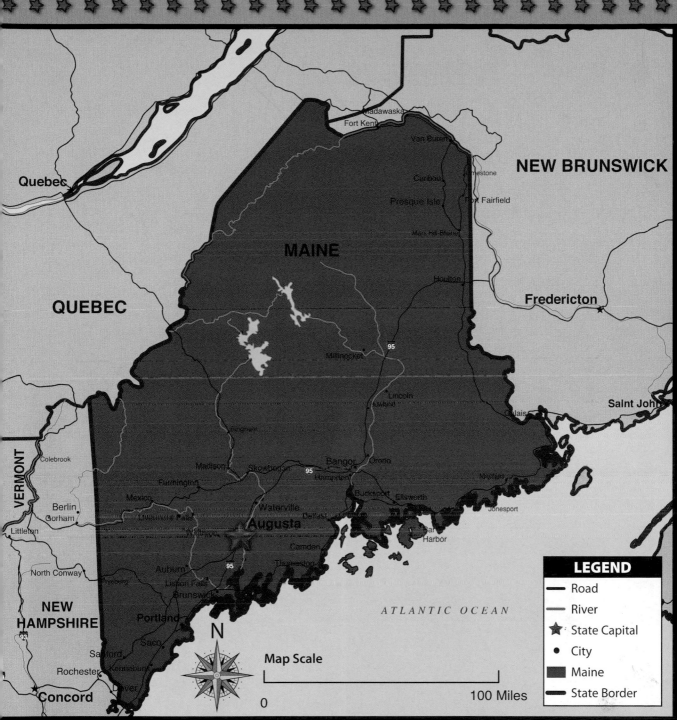

Madawaska
Fort Kent
Van Buren

NEW BRUNSWICK

Quebec

Caribou
Limestone

Presque Isle
Fort Fairfield

Mars Hill-Blaine

MAINE

Houlton

Fredericton

QUEBEC

95

Millinocket

Lincoln
Howland

Saint John

Calais

Bingham

Colebrook

Madison
Skowhegan
Bangor
Orono

95
Hampden
Machias

VERMONT

Farmington

Mexico

Waterville
Bucksport
Ellsworth

Berlin
Gorham

Livermore Falls
Delfast
Jonesport

Littleton

Winthrop
Augusta

Bar
Harbor

North Conway

Camden

ATLANTIC OCEAN

Auburn

95

Thomaston

Pryeburg
Lisbon Falls
Brunswick

NEW
HAMPSHIRE

Portland

N

93

Saco

Sanford
Kennebunk

Rochester

Map Scale

Dover

Concord

0

100 Miles

LEGEND

— Road
— River
★ State Capital
• City
▉ Maine
— State Border

United States

Hawai'i   Alaska

Maine

STATE CAPITAL

Augusta, established by traders from Plymouth Colony in 1628, is now the capital of Maine. Located on the Kennebec River, it is the most eastern capital city in the United States. Augusta was not the state's first capital. Portland served as the state capital until 1832.

The Land

Maine can be divided into three natural land regions. They are the Seaboard Lowland, the New England Upland, and the White Mountains Region. The Seaboard Lowland is a narrow region that stretches along Maine's Atlantic shoreline. The New England Upland region covers much of northern, eastern, and central Maine. It has hilly sections and level areas that are suitable for pastures and raising crops. Rivers, lakes, and **eskers** are also found in this region. The White Mountains Region extends from northern New Hampshire into Maine. It has the state's highest mountains and thickest forests.

CADILLAC MOUNTAIN

MOUNT KATAHDIN

The highest point in Maine is Mount Katahdin, located in the east-central part of the state. It rises 5,268 feet above sea level.

Approximately 1,200 islands dot the waters off Maine's coast. The largest island is Mount Desert Island. It is home to Acadia National Park's Cadillac Mountain, which measures 1,530 feet high.

MOOSEHEAD LAKE

The largest lake in Maine is Moosehead Lake. It covers 117 square miles.

SUGARLOAF MOUNTAIN

Maine has 14 peaks that rise above 4,000 feet, including Sugarloaf Mountain. At 4,237 feet, Sugarloaf Mountain is the state's second-highest peak.

Maine is the most heavily forested state in the United States. Trees cover more than 90 percent of its land area.

Aroostook County covers 6,672 square miles, making it the largest county in the United States east of the Mississippi River. Allagash Falls is part of this county.

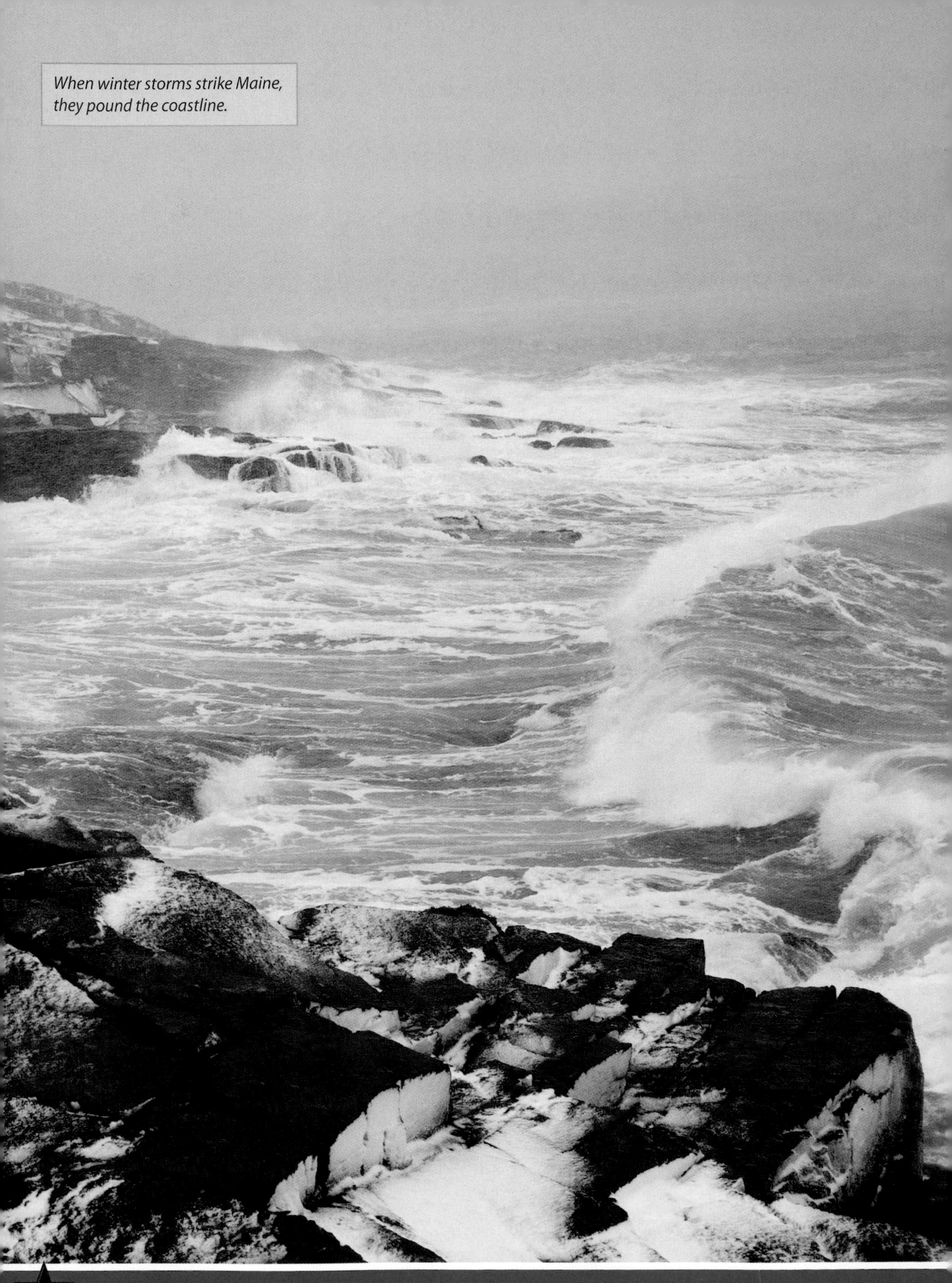

When winter storms strike Maine, they pound the coastline.

Climate

Maine experiences short summers and long, cold winters. The highest temperature ever recorded in the state was 105° Fahrenheit in North Bridgton on July 10, 1911. Maine's lowest recorded temperature was –48° F in Van Buren on January 19, 1925. The state typically has heavy snowfalls. Cold Arctic air collides with the warm air of the Gulf Stream to cause winter storms. In January 1998 an ice storm tore through the state. It was believed to be the worst natural disaster in Maine's history, and it left more than 800,000 people without electricity for several weeks.

Average Annual Precipitation Across Maine

Acadia National Park, Augusta, Portland, and Presque Isle all receive more than 35 inches of rain per year. Acadia National Park gets the most, with 57.3 inches of rainfall on average. Why might it rain more in one area of the state than another?

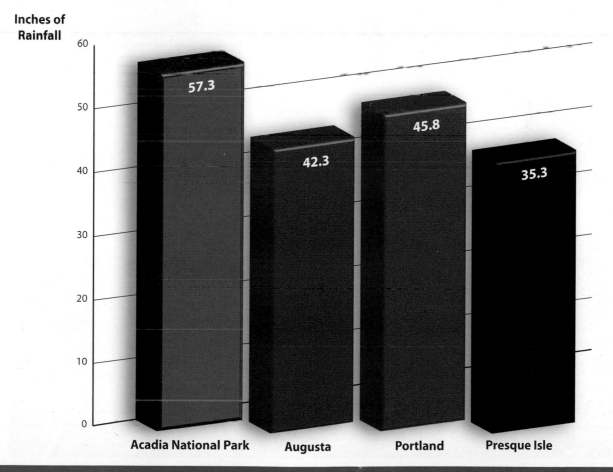

Inches of Rainfall

- Acadia National Park: 57.3
- Augusta: 42.3
- Portland: 45.8
- Presque Isle: 35.3

Natural Resources

T rees are one of Maine's most important natural resources. There are about 17 million acres of forest in the state. These forests supply raw materials for many of the wood products made in Maine. Private companies that harvest trees for lumber or paper production own much of Maine's forestland. Many companies use tree farming and eco-management to maintain forest resources. These methods help ensure that Maine's forests are preserved for future generations.

Throughout Maine mills process lumber into paper. Large paper mills operate in Millinocket, Jay, Skowhegan, and Rumford.

Water is another major natural resource in the state. Maine has more than 5,000 rivers and streams. Many of these rivers can be used to produce **hydroelectricity**. Hydroelectric dams are found on the state's four major rivers. These rivers are the Kennebec, the Penobscot, the Androscoggin, and the Saco. About 25 percent of Maine's power comes from hydroelectric plants. Maine also has about 6,000 lakes and ponds. The lakes and rivers support a variety of fish and marine life.

The Penobscot River empties into the Atlantic Ocean through Penobscot Bay. About 350 miles long, it is the state's longest river.

I DIDN'T KNOW THAT!

Maine's most valuable minerals are sand, gravel, and limestone.

The state gemstone is tourmaline. Often found in a type of granite called pegmatite, the crystal comes in a variety of colors, including blue, green, and black.

Maine's state tree is the white pine. The trunk of this tree was ideal for the construction of masts during the area's early shipbuilding days.

Plants

A great number of tree species are found in the state's vast forests. In the north, spruce and fir are plentiful. Elsewhere maple, birch, and white pine are common. Although private companies own most of Maine's forests, the state has several designated wilderness areas. One such area is Baxter State Park. Located in northern Maine, this park protects more than 200,000 acres of wilderness.

The state also has many colorful wildflowers, including asters, black-eyed Susans, and buttercups. Maine is known for the many lowbush blueberry plants that grow throughout the northern Seaboard Lowland.

FIR TREE

Fir trees have needlelike leaves. They are valued for their lumber and pulpwood.

MAPLE TREE

Maples trees come in many varieties and sizes. The leaves of maple trees usually turn beautiful colors in the fall.

LOWBUSH BLUEBERRIES

Lowbush blueberries, also known as wild blueberries, are native to North America. They grow close to the ground.

BLACK-EYED SUSANS

These common bright yellow flowers with dark centers grow on coarse, hairy stems. Black-eyed Susans bloom from June to August.

Irish moss grows along Maine's coast. This seaweed is gathered and processed into a substance called carrageenin. A thickening agent, carrageenin is used in foods such as ice cream, cheese, and salad dressing.

Apples, lowbush blueberries, strawberries, cranberries, and raspberries are valuable fruit crops in Maine.

Animals

Maine's forests and waters are home to a remarkable variety of wildlife. Among the state's many land animals are foxes, lynx, black bears, and porcupines. Approximately 30,000 moose, Maine's state mammal, roam the state. Moose are considered North America's tallest land mammal. They can often stand over 7 feet tall.

A wide range of marine life is found in Maine's coastal waters. Finback, humpback, and minke whales can all be seen in the Gulf of Maine. A minke whale has a curved dorsal fin and a white stripe on its flippers. Basking sharks and porpoises also live in these waters, as do a variety of shellfish such as lobsters, crabs, and shrimps. Among the many fish found in the state are haddock, cod, and mackerel. Harbor seals inhabit Maine's coastal waters.

HUMPBACK WHALE

Humpback whales are powerful swimmers that can leap out of the water with their massive fins. The mammals, which weigh about 40 tons, are endangered.

BLACK BEAR

Black bears weigh 200 to 600 pounds. They can be 6 feet long. Black bears can be shades of brown, but in Maine they are usually black.

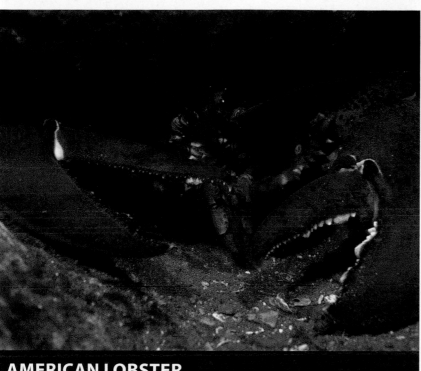

AMERICAN LOBSTER

American lobsters are caught commercially in Maine waters. They can grow up to 3.25 feet long and weigh often more than 5 pounds.

MOOSE

Some moose can weigh up to 1,800 pounds. Their antlers are typically more than 40 pounds.

The basking shark, which can be found in the Gulf of Maine, is the second-largest fish in the world. Only the whale shark is larger. Basking sharks often grow as long as 46 feet.

More than 300 bird species are found in Maine. They range from small birds, such as sparrows and blue jays, to predatory birds, such as eagles and hawks. The state also has many waterbirds, including ducks, loons, herons, cormorants, and terns. Atlantic puffins live off the coast of Maine.

Tourism

Sparkling lakes, rushing rivers, dense forests, towering mountains, and beautiful stretches of coastline all make Maine a natural paradise for vacationers. Many tourists travel to the state to enjoy the recreational activities offered by such wilderness areas as Baxter State Park, White Mountain National Forest, and the Allagash Wilderness Waterway. Tourists are also drawn to the state's seaside villages.

Mount Desert Island is a popular tourist destination in Maine. Charming communities, historic inns, and remote country roads can be found on the island. Acadia National Park encompasses nearly half of the island, as well as parts of the mainland. It offers a stunning landscape of rugged cliffs and rich woodlands. One of the most visited wonders in the park is a deep, coastal cavern called Thunder Hole. Seawater rushes into this cavern, compresses the air inside, and then bursts out with an explosive force to a height of 40 feet and a roar like the sound of thunder.

ACADIA NATIONAL PARK

Maine's coast has broad beaches, tiny fishing villages, and the only national park in New England, Acadia National Park.

MAINE MARITIME MUSEUM

At the Maine Maritime Museum in Bath, visitors can see paintings, ship models, and exhibits on life at sea. The museum also runs a boat builders day camp in the summer.

APPALACHIAN TRAIL

Many people who love the outdoors come to Maine to hike the Appalachian National Scenic Trail. The trail in Maine begins at Mount Katahdin.

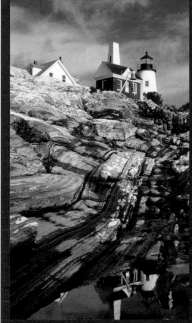

Pemaquid Point Light in Bristol was built in 1827. The tower is open to the public daily.

Portland is the site of the Children's Museum of Maine. This museum features a model space shuttle, animal hospital, grocery store, and sailboat.

Abbe Museum is dedicated to the preservation and celebration of Maine's American Indian communities. Its collections include more than 50,000 artifacts representing about 10,000 years of American Indian history. Originally located in Sieur de Monts Spring, the museum opened a second location in Bar Harbor in 2001.

ALLAGASH WILDERNESS WATERWAY

The Allagash Wilderness Waterway is a popular canoe route. It consists of a 92-mile corridor of lakes and rivers with many camping areas.

Industry

Maine's economy has long been linked to its abundant natural resources. In fact, one of the state's first industries was the cutting down of white pine trees. Trees continue to play an important role in the state's economy. They supply the raw materials for making paper products. The manufacture of paper is one of Maine's largest industries, and many major paper companies are based in the state.

Industries in Maine
Value of Goods and Services in Millions of Dollars

Maine's finance, insurance, and real estate industries generate the largest income for the state. Government, wholesale and retail trade, manufacturing, and health care follow in size. Why might the health care industry be so important?

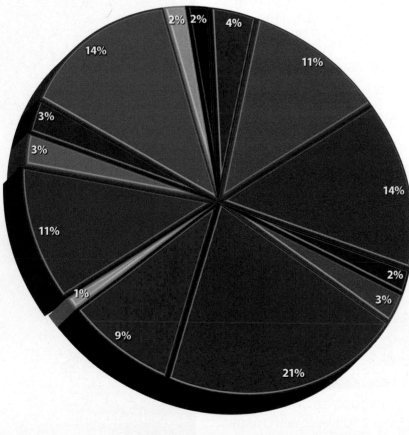

LEGEND

	Agriculture, Forestry, and Fishing	$777
*	Mining	$9
	Utilities	$904
	Construction	$2,141
	Manufacturing	$5,680
	Wholesale and Retail Trade	$6,889
	Transportation	$1,220
	Media and Entertainment	$1,775
	Finance, Insurance, and Real Estate	$10,584
	Professional and Technical Services	$4,670
	Education	$587
	Health Care	$5,653
	Hotels and Restaurants	$1,698
	Other Services	$1,317
	Government	$7,104
TOTAL		**$51,008**

*Less than 1%. Percentages may not add to 100 because of rounding.

Maine's trees are also harvested for the manufacture of lumber. Logging camps and sawmills are found in the state. Wood products manufactured in Maine include clothespins, lobster traps, matches, and boats. About 90 percent of all the toothpicks used in the United States are made in Maine.

Fishing is another notable industry in the state. Maine's waters provide profitable catches of fish and shellfish. About 90 percent of the country's lobster supply is caught in the coastal waters of Maine. Other catches include ocean perch, sea herring, cod, clams, sea scallops, and shrimps.

Fishers in Maine are required to use lobster traps. In Maine it is illegal to drag a net across the ocean floor to catch lobsters because it damages other ocean life.

I DIDN'T KNOW THAT!

The first sawmill in what is now the United States was constructed near York. It began operations in 1623.

Shipbuilding was once one of Maine's most important industries. The town of Bath is still known as the City of Ships. The Bath Iron Works builds ships for the U.S. Navy.

Llamas and alpacas raised in Maine are used for breeding, carrying goods, and cart pulling. They are also considered good guard animals and can protect sheep and cattle.

American Indians

Archaeological discoveries in Maine have led scientists to believe that people were living in the area more than 10,000 years ago. These early people probably hunted caribou and other large animals that are no longer found in Maine.

Another group emerged in Maine about 6,000 years ago. They are known as the Red Paint People because of their fascinating burial practices. They lined burial pits with bright red **ochre** and then placed unusual stone tools and weapons in the pits before burying their dead. The Red Paint People thrived in the area until about 1800 BC.

The Penobscot people have lived in what is now Maine for thousands of years.

Some Penobscot Indians in Maine continue to practice traditions such as building birchbark canoes.

When Europeans began to establish settlements in Maine in the early 1600s, several groups of American Indians were living in the region. Most belonged to the Abenaki confederation, including the Penobscot and the Passamaquoddy. The American Indians lost much of the land to the Europeans. In 1980 the U.S. government agreed to pay $81.5 million to Maine's Passamaquoddy and Penobscot. The money was payment for land illegally taken in the 1700s and 1800s.

I DIDN'T KNOW THAT!

The word *Abenaki* comes from an Algonquian word meaning "People of the First Light."

Scientists believe that when Europeans began settling in the Maine region, the Abenaki population was as high as 20,000. However, by 1620 this number was cut by more than half due to new diseases introduced and spread by the settlers.

American Indian tribes formed the Abenaki confederation to protect themselves from Iroquois tribes, especially the Mohawk. The Iroquois were enemies of the Abenaki and would often raid Abenaki villages.

The Passamaquoddy and Penobscot each have seats in Maine's House of Representatives, and they speak on tribal matters. A Passamaquoddy named Peter Moore served as an American Indian delegate in Maine in 1931.

Explorers

It is not known when the first European explorers reached Maine. Some historians believe that Vikings, led by Leif Eriksson, visited Maine in about AD 1000. However, there is little evidence to support this assertion. There is also some doubt about whether an expedition led by the Italian explorer John Cabot reached the Maine coast in the late 1490s. Cabot's son, Sebastian, who was part of the expedition, claimed that they had sailed Maine's coast. Unfortunately, records kept during the expedition were unclear, leading many historians to question Sebastian's claim.

There is no doubt, however, that an Italian explorer named Giovanni da Verrazzano visited the region in the early 1500s. Sailing on behalf of France, Verrazzano arrived on Maine's coast in 1524 but soon left the area. Verrazzano called the region "the land of the bad people" because the American Indians he encountered there were not friendly. Soon after, European fishers discovered Maine's excellent coastal fishing grounds, and more ships began to frequent the area's waters.

Italian navigator John Cabot, in the service of England, traveled across the Atlantic Ocean to the coast of North America in the late 1490s. He landed at what is now southern Nova Scotia or perhaps Maine.

Timeline of Settlement

Early Exploration

1000 Vikings, led by Leif Eriksson, may have visited what is now Maine for the first time.

1524 Italian explorer Giovanni da Verrazzano, sailing on behalf of France, arrives on the coast of what is today Maine.

Colonization

1604 The French establish a colony on Saint Croix Island.

1607 English colonists establish Popham Colony on the Kennebec River.

1622 The Council for New England, charged with colonizing and governing the area, grants Maine to Englishman Sir Ferdinando Gorges.

Growth

1641 Gorgeana, now called York, becomes the first chartered city in the country.

1658 Maine officially becomes part of Massachusetts.

American Revolution and Civil War

1775–1783 Hundreds of Maine residents join the American Revolution. The war ends in the creation of the United States.

1819 Voters in Maine choose to separate from Massachusetts.

1820 Maine becomes the 23rd state to enter the Union.

1832 Augusta replaces Portland as Maine's capital.

1861–1865 People from Maine fight for the Union in the Civil War.

Early Settlers

At the beginning of the 1600s both France and England attempted to establish colonies in Maine. In 1604 the French explorers Pierre du Guast and Samuel de Champlain led an expedition to form a colony on Saint Croix Island. However, the winter was very harsh, and in 1605 the settlers left the area.

Map of Settlements and Resources in Early Maine

4 *English colonists established Popham Colony on the Kennebec River in 1607. They abandoned the settlement in less than a year after a severe winter during which several colonists died.*

1 *The Shakers, a religious group, founded settlements in New England in the 1700s. Today Maine is home to Sabbathday Lake Shaker Community, the last active Shaker community in the world, near New Gloucester.*

5 *In 1613 a French Jesuit mission was established on Mount Desert Island. That same year, however, an English captain discovered the mission and destroyed it. He also destroyed other French settlements in the area.*

2 *The state's many pine trees have contributed to its lumber and shipbuilding industries since the 1700s.*

6 *Maine's beaver population brought French and English fur traders to the region in the early 1600s. Europeans traded items such as guns and kettles with the Abenaki for beaver pelts and other furs.*

3 *Since the early 1600s when European settlers came to what is now Maine, the ocean waters have provided fish and shellfish, including lobster, to the population.*

Scale

0   100 Miles

N

LEGEND

Settlement		Seafood	
River		Maine	
Fur		State Border	
Wood			

In 1606 an English trading company called the Plymouth Company was granted Maine and other areas for colonization. The following year it sent colonists to the Kennebec River to settle Popham Colony, which was named in honor of its leader, George Popham. After a terrible winter, these colonists abandoned the settlement in 1608.

In 1622 the Council for New England, charged with colonizing and governing the area, granted Maine and New Hampshire to the Englishmen Sir Ferdinando Gorges and John Mason. The two men divided the area in 1629, and Gorges received what is today Maine. Beginning in the early 1620s, a number of permanent settlements were established, including Saco and Kittery. In 1641 Gorgeana became the first chartered city in the country. Some 10 years later it was renamed York.

Land disputes between England and France erupted into violent battles. From the early 1600s to the mid-1700s the two powers fought many wars for control of Maine and the rest of eastern North America. In 1763 this turmoil came to an end with the **Treaty** of Paris. The treaty called for France to surrender almost all of its North American territories east of the Mississippi River. Very soon after the treaty, Britain decided to increase taxes on its American colonies and restrict their trade. These actions caused severe unrest among the colonists, and many decided to fight for their independence. In 1775 hundreds of Maine residents joined the American Revolution.

When the colonists emerged victorious in 1783, 13 colonies came together to form the United States. At that time Maine was part of Massachusetts, but a movement for separation began to gain strength. In 1819 Maine voted in favor of separation. On March 15, 1820, with a population of about 300,000 people, Maine entered the Union as the 23rd state.

I DIDN'T KNOW THAT!

The settlers of Popham Colony built the *Virginia* so that they could sail home to England. It was the first ship built in the United States. In 2007, shipbuilders in Bath constructed parts of a replica of the ship.

Englishman Sir Ferdinando Gorges spent most of his adult life developing colonies in New England, but he never actually set foot in North America.

Maine remained a part of Massachusetts for almost 150 years.

Maine's admission to the Union was part of the Missouri **Compromise**. This agreement allowed Maine to enter the Union as a **free state** and Missouri to enter as a slave state. This kept the number of free and slave states equal.

Notable People

Many notable people have contributed to the development of the 23rd state to join the Union. A European explorer found and claimed the land for France in the 1500s. An Abenaki chief then helped English colonists in the region. Much later, celebrated authors of poetry, children's stories, and science fiction wrote imaginatively about Maine and rest of the world around them. And throughout the years, political leaders have worked to help Maine and its people prosper.

GIOVANNI DA VERRAZZANO
(1485–1528)

Italian navigator Verrazzano was likely the first European to explore what is now Maine. France had sent Verrazzano to the find a westward passage to Asia in 1524, but he found North America instead and claimed Maine for France. He died in 1528.

SAMOSET
(c. 1590–c. 1653)

Samoset, born in what is now southeastern Maine in about 1590, was an Abenaki chief who had learned English and helped negotiate a treaty between the Plymouth colonists and the Wampanaog in what is now Massachusetts. He also helped the colonists to prosper in their new land. Samoset died in about 1653.

HENRY WADSWORTH LONGFELLOW (1807–1882)

Poet Longfellow was in born in Portland and attended Bowdoin College. He wrote many famous ballads, including "Paul Revere's Ride," and *The Song of Hiawatha* (1855). Longfellow's long poem *Evangeline* (1847) traces the story of the Acadians and their expulsion from Nova Scotia, Canada.

MARGARET CHASE SMITH (1897–1995)

Born in Skowhegan, Smith was the first woman to serve in both houses of the U.S. Congress. She served in the House of Representatives from 1940 to 1949 and in the Senate from 1949 to 1973. Smith, known as "the conscience of the Senate," died in Skowhegan, the city of her birth, in 1995.

GEORGE HERBERT WALKER BUSH (1924–)

Bush was the country's 41st president, from 1989 to 1993. He was born in Milton, Massachusetts, but he has spent summers at the family estate in Kennebunkport since he was a child. During his presidency, he often hosted world leaders there. His eldest son, George W. Bush, was the 43rd U.S. president.

E. B. White (1899–1985) spent many of his summers at Penobscot Bay. White is perhaps best known for his popular children's novels *Stuart Little* (1945), *The Trumpet of the Swan* (1970), and *Charlotte's Web* (1952).

Stephen King (1947–) was born in Portland in 1947, and the best-selling author continues to live and write in Maine. Many of his enormously popular novels have been made into films. Among his many bestsellers are *The Shining*, *Pet Sematary*, and *It*.

Population

Maine is home to more than 1.3 million people. The majority of the state's people live in towns or communities with populations of fewer than 2,500. Only about two-fifths of Maine's people live in urban areas. This makes Maine one of the few states in the country where the rural population is more numerous than the urban population. The cities are small. Portland, with about 63,000 people, is Maine's largest city. Among the state's other largest cities are Lewiston, Bangor, South Portland, Auburn, Brunswick, Biddeford, and Augusta. Much of the population lives in the southwest corner of Maine, leaving large portions of the state sparsely inhabited.

Maine Population 1950–2010

Maine's population has grown in every decade since 1950, but not by large amounts. What contributes to the slow growth of a state's population?

Number of People

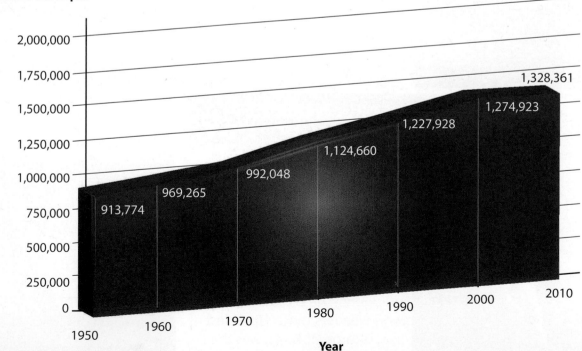

913,774 (1950)
969,265 (1960)
992,048 (1970)
1,124,660 (1980)
1,227,928 (1990)
1,274,923 (2000)
1,328,361 (2010)

Year

The most populated counties in Maine are Cumberland, York, Penobscot, and Kennebec.

The people of Maine are sometimes called Down Easters, a term that is also given to the harsh winds and tides that come in along the Atlantic coast.

There are five federally recognized Indian tribes in Maine today.

Maine has about 43 residents per square mile. It is one of the country's smaller states by population.

Most of Maine's residents live in the countryside, outside the state's cities.

About 97 percent of the people living in Maine were born in the United States, and most are of European descent. People with English ancestry are by far the largest cultural group in Maine. However, people of French, Irish, French Canadian, German, and Scottish descent are also present in significant numbers.

Workers laid the cornerstone of the Maine State House in Augusta in 1829.

Politics and Government

Maine's government is made up of three branches. The legislative branch makes the state's laws. It consists of the Senate, which has 35 members, and the House of Representatives, which has 151 members. All members are elected to two-year terms. The executive branch of government ensures that the laws are carried out. This branch is headed by a governor who is elected to a four-year term. The governor is the only member of the executive branch who is elected by the people. Other members are chosen by the legislature or appointed by the governor with approval from the Senate. The third branch of government is the judicial branch. It interprets the state's laws and ensures that they are obeyed. The highest court in Maine is the Supreme Judicial Court.

Maine has 16 counties, 22 cities, and 424 incorporated towns. Town government, with the annual town meeting and a board of selectmen, prevails in most communities.

The state government and its various departments have many responsibilities, including issuing badges to Maine's registered guides. All guides must pass a test to lead others in natural areas in the state.

Cultural Groups

Maine's people come from a variety of cultural backgrounds. The first Europeans to establish permanent settlements in Maine came from England. They were soon joined by colonists who migrated to Maine from other states and by Scots-Irish settlers. Together the English and the Scots-Irish made up the largest portion of Maine's population during its early settlement days.

People of French descent make up the second largest cultural group in Maine. In 1763 the English expelled French settlers, called Acadians, from Nova Scotia, Canada. Many of them established homes in the St. John Valley. In the 1800s French Canadians from Quebec moved to Maine to find jobs in the lumber and textile mills. Today Maine's Acadian culture is recognized at the Acadian Village in Van Buren. It features a number of reconstructed and relocated buildings that depict early Acadian life in the St. John Valley. Among the buildings on display are a country schoolhouse, a blacksmith shop, and a chapel.

French Canadian migrants built Saint Mary's Church, now the Franco-American Heritage Center, in Lewiston. Work began in 1907 and took 20 years to complete.

A Penobscot community lives on Indian Island in the Penobscot River.

In the mid-1800s people in Maine began to move westward to other states. In an effort to keep settlement numbers high, Maine's commissioner of immigration brought a group of 51 Swedish immigrants to the area in 1870. These immigrants established a settlement in Aroostook County that grew into the township of New Sweden. Soon the Swedish townships of Westmanland and Stockholm were established close by. Many descendants of these early Swedish settlers continue to live in these communities. Historic sites in New Sweden include an original log house, blacksmith shop, and one-room schoolhouse. Every summer the community of New Sweden celebrates and shares its heritage with the Midsommar Celebration. The festival features Swedish food, music, and dancing.

Before any Europeans settled in Maine, many American Indians called the area home. Today many of their descendants still live in the state. The Passamaquoddy live mostly on two reservations in Washington County, while the Penobscot live on Indian Island. There are also small populations of Micmac and Malecite in Maine.

Many Italians, Russians, Poles, Finns, and other European settlers came to Maine in the 1800s to work in the state's lumber and textile mills.

French is the primary language spoken in much of the St. John Valley, and it is the second language most commonly spoken in many of Maine's cities.

Every summer the town of Madawaska celebrates Acadian heritage with a festival, which has become one of the largest cultural events in Maine. Visitors to Madawaska can also see Acadian carvings from about 1912.

The Greek Heritage Festival is held every July in the town of Saco. This three-day event celebrates Greek heritage with Greek food and dancing.

Arts and Entertainment

Maine's beauty has served as an inspiration for many poets and novelists. Henry Wadsworth Longfellow is considered to be one of the country's most influential poets. He was born in Portland in 1807. Edna St. Vincent Millay was another popular poet from Maine. She was born in Rockland in 1892. In 1923 she received a Pulitzer Prize for a volume of poetry titled *Ballad of the Harp-Weaver*.

Respected novelists born in Maine include Kenneth Roberts and Sarah Orne Jewett. One of the country's most popular **contemporary** novelists is also from the state. Maine-born Stephen King is a longtime resident of Bangor. He is known for his chilling horror novels featuring ordinary characters who must battle evil forces. Numerous other writers have lived in the state as well. These include Harriet Beecher Stowe and May Sarton.

Edna St. Vincent Millay produced poetry, essays, and verse plays. She was inspired by the coast and the landscapes of her home state of Maine.

In 1963, Andrew Wyeth became the first painter ever awarded the Presidential Medal of Freedom. He died in 2009 at the age of 91.

Maine's stunning natural scenery has also inspired many visual artists. Renowned painters, such as Thomas Cole, Winslow Homer, Rockwell Kent, Edward Hopper, and Andrew Wyeth, have all captured on canvas the state's peaceful way of life and its rugged, beautiful landscapes. Other artists have represented Maine's beauty through photographs, sculptures, and craftwork. Many of the works produced in Maine are on display in museums, such as the Portland Museum of Art and the Bowdoin College Museum of Art in Brunswick.

Exciting theatrical performances and musical events take place in Maine each year. Maine is also home to a wide range of talented musical groups, from barbershop quartets to choral music choirs. The state hosts a number of festivals that celebrate a variety of musical styles. The Saltwater Music Festival in Brunswick is noted for the diversity of its performers, who have included country, folk, and jazz musicians. The Blistered Fingers Family Bluegrass Music Festival in Sidney is a popular event for the whole family.

I DIDN'T KNOW THAT!

Harriet Beecher Stowe wrote her first novel, *Uncle Tom's Cabin*, while living in Brunswick. Published in 1852, this antislavery masterpiece is often said to have helped start the American Civil War.

Milton Bradley, who was born in Vienna in 1836, founded a popular children's game company. Its products include Life, Scrabble, Twister, and Chutes and Ladders.

Lillian Nordica was a prominent opera singer during the late 1800s and early 1900s. She was born in Farmington and was nicknamed the Lily of the North by her fans.

Actor Patrick Dempsey was born in Lewiston in 1966. He has starred in the television series *Grey's Anatomy* and the films *Enchanted* and *Valentine's Day*.

Sports

A variety of water sports may be enjoyed in Maine's coastal waters, lakes, and rivers. Sea kayakers paddle along the state's beautiful coastline and explore the offshore islands and protected **estuaries**. Surfers are also attracted to Maine's coast. The area's large, crashing **breakers** provide excellent challenges for experienced surfers. Beautiful ocean beaches in the southern part of the state buzz with activity. These coastal waters can be quite chilly, and swimming in them is not for everyone. Warmer waters are found in Maine's lakes. Other water sports enjoyed in Maine include canoeing, white-water rafting, and **windjamming**.

Excellent hiking and biking trails are found in Maine's mountains and forests. One of the most popular hikes is the Appalachian National Scenic Trail, which begins in Maine at Mount Katahdin. This trail winds for more than 2,100 miles through the Appalachian Mountains and crosses 14 states. The Maine section of the Appalachian Trail has steep climbs and dense woods that provide a great hiking challenge.

Kayaking in the Penobscot Bay appeals to residents and visitors alike.

Although winter in Maine is usually long and cold, many sports enthusiasts consider it to be the state's best season. Once the first few snowfalls have blanketed the state, Maine's hiking and biking trails turn into excellent areas for snowshoeing, snowmobiling, and cross-country skiing. Ice skating and ice fishing are popular activities when Maine's lakes and ponds have frozen over, and frozen waterfalls provide slippery challenges for ice climbers.

Downhill skiing is probably Maine's most popular winter sport. The two major ski resorts are Sugarloaf and Sunday River. Both have a variety of runs that are suitable for skiers and snowboarders of all ability levels. Among the state's other great hills are Shawnee Peak, Saddleback, Big Rock, and Mount Abram. Maine's hills play host to a variety of ski and snowboard events. In 2006, Seth Wescott of Carrabassett Valley became the first man to win Olympic gold in snowboard cross, which is a group race on snowboards. He won gold again in 2010.

Snowboarder Seth Wescott overcame a long-term injury and a disappointing qualifying run to win a gold medal at the 2010 Vancouver Winter Olympics.

The Annual Maine Potato Blossom Festival at Fort Fairfield features unique athletic events such as potato-picking contests and mashed-potato wrestling.

Portland is home to a popular Double-A baseball team. The Portland Sea Dogs play at Hadlock Field.

Maine's first licensed hunting guide was a woman named Cornelia Thurza Crosby. She was affectionately known as Fly Rod because of her amazing knack for fly-fishing. Crosby once caught 200 trout in just one day.

Snowmobiling is a very popular sport in Maine. The state has hundreds of snowmobile clubs.

Maine's state fish is the landlocked salmon. This fish lives in Maine's lakes and rivers and attracts many sport fishers to the state every year.

After breaking her leg skiing as a teenager, Joan Benoit Samuelson took up running to get back in shape. In 1979, the senior at Bowdoin College won the Boston Marathon. Samuelson went on to win the first Olympic women's marathon in 1984.

National Averages Comparison

The United States is a federal republic, consisting of fifty states and the District of Columbia. Alaska and Hawai'i are the only non-contiguous, or non-touching, states in the nation. Today, the United States of America is the third-largest country in the world in population. The United States Census Bureau takes a census, or count of all the people, every ten years. It also regularly collects other kinds of data about the population and the economy. How does Maine compare with the national average?

Comparison Chart

United States 2010 Census Data *	USA	Maine
Admission to Union	NA	March 15, 1820
Land Area (in square miles)	3,537,438.44	30,861.55
Population Total	308,745,538	1,328,361
Population Density (people per square mile)	87.28	43.04
Population Percentage Change (April 1, 2000, to April 1, 2010)	9.7%	4.2%
White Persons (percent)	72.4%	95.2%
Black Persons (percent)	12.6%	1.2%
American Indian and Alaska Native Persons (percent)	0.9%	0.6%
Asian Persons (percent)	4.8%	1.0%
Native Hawaiian and Other Pacific Islander Persons (percent)	0.2%	—
Some Other Race (percent)	6.2%	0.3%
Persons Reporting Two or More Races (percent)	2.9%	1.6%
Persons of Hispanic or Latino Origin (percent)	16.3%	1.3%
Not of Hispanic or Latino Origin (percent)	83.7%	98.7%
Median Household Income	$52,029	$46,419
Percentage of People Age 25 or Over Who Have Graduated from High School	80.4%	85.4%

*All figures are based on the 2010 United States Census, with the exception of the last two items. Percentages may not add to 100 because of rounding.

How to Improve My Community

Strong communities make strong states. Think about what features are important in your community. What do you value? Education? Health? Forests? Safety? Beautiful spaces? Government works to help citizens create ideal living conditions that are fair to all by providing services in communities. Consider what changes you could make in your community. How would they improve your state as a whole? Using this concept web as a guide, write a report that outlines the features you think are most important in your community and what improvements could be made. A strong state needs strong communities.

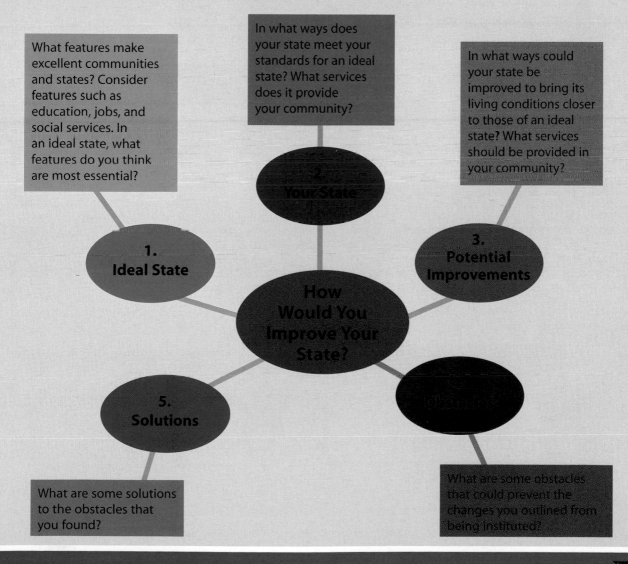

What features make excellent communities and states? Consider features such as education, jobs, and social services. In an ideal state, what features do you think are most essential?

In what ways does your state meet your standards for an ideal state? What services does it provide your community?

In what ways could your state be improved to bring its living conditions closer to those of an ideal state? What services should be provided in your community?

2.
Your State

1.
Ideal State

3.
Potential Improvements

How Would You Improve Your State?

5.
Solutions

What are some solutions to the obstacles that you found?

What are some obstacles that could prevent the changes you outlined from being instituted?

Exercise Your Mind!

Think about these questions and then use your research skills to find the answers and learn more fascinating facts about Maine. A teacher, librarian, or parent may be able to help you locate the best sources to use in your research.

1 True or False: Earmuffs were invented in Maine.

2 One of the landmarks in Kennebunk is a house that was constructed to resemble a:

a. Boat
b. Pine Tree
c. Wedding Cake
d. Shoe

3 True or False: Maine has produced one of the world's greatest marathon runners.

4 True or False: Augusta has always been the capital of Maine.

5 How many politicians from Maine have served as vice president of the United States?

a. Zero
b. Two
c. Five
d. Seven

6 True or False: The United States and Canada almost went to war over disputes concerning Maine's border with New Brunswick.

7 What Maine city has been known as Machigonne, Elbow, The Neck, Casco, and Falmouth over the years?

8 True or False: Lobster has been used as fertilizer in Maine.

Words to Know

allocates: sets something, such as money, aside for a particular purpose

breakers: waves that break into foam

compromise: a settlement

contemporary: modern or in the present-day

eskers: winding ridges of gravel and other sediment, formed by glacial meltwater

estuaries: the tidal area where a river meets the sea

free state: a state where slavery is not permitted

hydroelectricity: electricity generated by the power of moving water

ochre: clay that is orange or red in color

treaty: an agreement

windjamming: sailing on a large ship

Index

Acadia National Park 10, 13, 20
Acadians 33, 38, 39
American Indians 4, 21, 25, 26, 27, 28, 32, 35, 39
American Revolution 29, 31
Appalachian National Scenic Trail 21, 42
Atlantic Ocean 6, 7, 8, 10, 35
Augusta 9, 13, 25, 34

Bangor 34, 40
Bath 20, 23, 31
Baxter State Park 16, 20
blueberries 16, 17, 24
Brunswick 34, 41
Bush, George Herbert Walker 32, 33

Cabot, John 28
Cabot, Sebastian 28
Cadillac Mountain 10

Champlain, Samuel de 30

Dempsey, Patrick 41

Eriksson, Leif 28, 29

Gorges, Sir Ferdinando 29, 31

Kennebec River 9, 15, 25, 29, 30, 31
King, Stephen 33, 40

lobster 18, 19, 23, 30,
Longfellow, Henry Wadsworth 32, 33, 40

Maine Maritime Academy 25
Millay, Edna St. Vincent 40
moose 18, 19
Mount Desert Island 10, 20, 30
Mount Katahdin 10, 21, 42

New England Upland 10

Penobscot River 15
Popham Colony 29, 30, 31
Portland 7, 9, 13, 21, 24, 25, 29, 33, 34, 40, 41, 43
potatoes 24, 43
puffins 19

Samoset 32
Seaboard Lowland 10, 16
Smith, Margaret Chase 32, 33
Stowe, Harriet Beecher 40, 41

Verrazzano, Giovanni da 28, 29 32

Wescott, Seth 43
White, E. B. 33
White Mountains Region 10
Wyeth, Andrew 41

Log on to www.av2books.com

AV² by Weigl brings you media enhanced books that support active learning. Go to www.av2books.com, and enter the special code found on page 2 of this book. You will gain access to enriched and enhanced content that supplements and complements this book. Content includes video, audio, web links, quizzes, a slide show, and activities.

Audio
Listen to sections of the book read aloud.

Video
Watch informative video clips.

Embedded Weblinks
Gain additional information for research.

Try This!
Complete activities and hands-on experiments.

WHAT'S ONLINE?

Try This!	Embedded Weblinks	Video	EXTRA FEATURES
Test your knowledge of the state in a mapping activity.	Discover more attractions in Maine.	Watch a video introduction to Maine.	**Audio** Listen to sections of the book read aloud.
Find out more about temperature or precipitation in your city.	Learn more about the history of the state.	Watch a video about the features of the state.	**Key Words** Study vocabulary, and complete a matching word activity.
Plan what attractions you would like to visit in the state.	Learn the full lyrics of the state song.		**Slide Show** View images and captions, and prepare a presentation.
Learn more about the early natural resources of the state.			**Quizzes** Test your knowledge.
Write a biography about a notable resident of Maine.			
Complete an educational census activity.			

AV² was built to bridge the gap between print and digital. We encourage you to tell us what you like and what you want to see in the future.

Sign up to be an AV² Ambassador at www.av2books.com/ambassador.

Due to the dynamic nature of the Internet, some of the URLs and activities provided as part of AV² by Weigl may have changed or ceased to exist. AV² by Weigl accepts no responsibility for any such changes. All media enhanced books are regularly monitored to update addresses and sites in a timely manner. Contact AV² by Weigl at 1-866-649-3445 or av2books@weigl.com with any questions, comments, or feedback.